LEARN HOW TO
CANOE IN ONE DAY

10850079

Learn How to Canoe in One Day

Quickest Way to Start Paddling,
Turning, Portaging, and Maintaining

Robert Birkby

Illustrations by Barbara Lien

Photographs by Kate Joost

Stackpole Books

Copyright © 1990 by Robert Birkby

Published by
STACKPOLE BOOKS
Cameron and Kelker Streets
P.O. Box 1831
Harrisburg, PA 17105

Printed in the United States of America

10   9   8   7   6   5   4   3   2   1

First Edition

Interior design by Marcia Lee Dobbs

Library of Congress Cataloging-in-Publication Data
Birkby, Robert.
   Learn how to canoe in one day : quickest way to
start paddling, turning, portaging, and maintaining /
Robert Birkby ; illustrations by Barbara Lien ;
photographs by Kate Joost.
      p.   cm.
   Includes index.
   ISBN 0-8117-2249-X
   1. Canoes and canoeing.   I. Title.
GV783.B54   1990   89-34189
797.1'22—dc20   CIP

And it floated on the river
Like a yellow leaf in Autumn
Like a yellow water lily.

Longfellow,
The Song of Hiawatha

Among all the modes of progression hitherto invented by
restless man, there is not one that
can compare in respect of comfort and luxury with travelling in
a birchbark canoe. It is the
poetry of progression.

The Earl of Dunraven

Don't for a moment imagine
there is anything difficult in
learning to handle a canoe: THE
FIRST LESSON ON A BICYCLE
IS UNBELIEVABLY DIFFICULT
BY COMPARISON.

R. H. McCarthy, Canoeing

Contents

Why Canoe?

Imagine yourself far from home, paddling a canoe across a wilderness lake. The sun warms your face, and the breeze bears the scent of evergreens lining the shore. With a rhythmic swing of your shoulders and arms, you ease your canoe in a graceful glide toward open country. There is no sound except the dip of the paddle and the soft rush of water breaking against the bow.

Or think what it would be like on a sweltering summer day to launch a canoe on the lake of a city park and paddle away from the noise, the heat, and the crowds. You might push off from shore and paddle furiously for a while, reveling in the joy of motion and the refreshing release of honest

You can learn to canoe in one day!

effort. Or you may simply drift, carried along by the current.

Perhaps you have tried canoeing, but found the experience anything but refreshing. Despite your best efforts with the paddle, the canoe seemed impossible to steer. You went around in circles for a while, feared the craft would capsize at any moment, and finally went home tired and disillusioned.

I can assure you that with a little guidance, you can canoe. There is no great mystery to it, no secret art beyond your grasp. In fact, you can become a fairly good quiet-water canoeist in just eight hours. Devote one day to it, and you'll master more of the canoeing art than many paddlers learn in a lifetime.

If that doesn't convince you to take to the water, here are a few more reasons to go canoeing.

- Canoeing is a sport for people of all ages and abilities. It need not be physically demanding, though if you want it to, canoeing can provide all the athletic challenge you can handle.
- Canoeing is a fine alternative to costly, crowded recreational activities. You can discover simple pleasures on almost any body of water. It is ideal for fishing, camping, bird watching, and back-country exploration. Able to follow nearly any watery pathway, a canoe is the ultimate off-road vehicle. It burns no fuel, emits no fumes, and

does nothing to foul the water or the air. In many parts of the country, the equipment you'll need can be rented at very reasonable rates.

- Canoes are lightweight and, if you know a few basic principles, easy to manage. The design is as clean, elegant, and functional as any creation of man. Long, slender shapes help keep canoes on course as they glide across the water. Riding high on the waves, they can carry heavy loads. When there is no water, you can hoist a canoe onto your shoulders and walk it to the next lake or stream.

- Finally, there is what might be called the Zen of canoeing—the act of perfecting a skill for the sheer joy of mastering it, keeping it alive, and learning from it. Since the introduction of outboard motors, the ability to handle a canoe hasn't been a vital necessity for very many people. Given the option of riding in a speedboat, many folks would scoff at someone who chooses instead to go in a canoe. Paddling across the water can seem as outdated as churning butter by hand, cutting timber with a crosscut saw, or splitting fence rails with an ax.

Yet, in the quick, silent flow of a canoe, you may feel yourself regaining control over the direction you are moving, both in the outdoors and in your life. Rather than relying on the vagaries of a snorting engine, you can depend upon your own strength and finesse to power your travels. Liberated from the shore and from the usual demands and inconveniences of modern life, you can find an exhilarating freedom. Canoeing offers a gentle fusion of physical exertion and outdoor discovery, of meditation and quiet motion.

Of his canoe, author Orange Frazer wrote in 1883, "I received it fresh from the hands of its maker, bright and new, its sides and deck polished and glistening until they reflected the sunbeams like a mirror, and its shape so graceful that it seemed about to metamorphose itself into a living swan and paddle away, even on dry land, on its own account."

After he had paddled his canoe a while, Frazer exclaimed, "What an attachment springs up between man and canoe in the course of a long, solitary cruise! Together you have travelled through the bright sunshine and the pelting rain; together floated down past the flower-crowned banks of the rivers, and by the grand scenery of the mountain gaps; together run the swift, exciting rapids, crossed the great lakes, fought the storm, and maybe together you have been rocked in the mighty wave-cradle of Old Ocean itself."

Try canoeing and sense the rare delight paddlers like Orange Frazer have come to know so well. Canoeing is an activity for an afternoon and a sport for a lifetime. You can learn how to canoe in one day, then enjoy many years refining your skill.

Of course, you'll want to start out right so you can canoe safely and well. This book will show you how.

Paddling out of the Past

If there is a classic American vessel of travel, it is the canoe. It is an American invention, coming down to us through the ages, better and more useful as generation after generation of builders refined the basic design.

In an 1887 *Outing Magazine* article on the history of American canoeing, C. Bowyer Vaux wrote that "The pale-faces who discovered America found the bark canoe a fact, complete and perfect—and they could not improve it; nor did they try. Thus has the bark canoe come down to us, floating on the flood of years—centuries—practically the same boat that it was when first discovered in the hands of the Indian by the white man."

Where trees grew large, craftsmen of old burned and hewed out the hearts of logs, then carved them into boats. These dugouts came to be known as *pirogues* on the islands of the Caribbean and in the swamplands and marshes of the South. Their low, slender shapes made them ideal for still waters.

In the Pacific Northwest, Haida Indians felled towering cedars and hewed them into great, high-sided canoes with steep prows that could slash through the surf of the ocean and the waves of stormy inlets and sounds.

Further north, Eskimos fashioned kayak frames from driftwood and bone, then stretched the cured skins of seals over them. They stitched the skins together with thongs and caulked the seams with tallow.

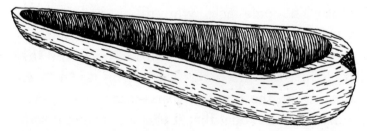

Carved from logs, dugouts and pirogues are the forefathers of today's canoes.

Early European explorers nearing the east coast of America reported their fascination at being greeted by natives in canoes made of bark. The craft moved lightly across the water and could easily outdistance the rowboats the explorers lowered to go ashore. Unlike the sailors facing the sterns of the dinghies in order to pull the oars, the Indian paddlers faced forward, giving them the decided advantage of being able to see where they were going.

Across the great North Country and well into what would become Canada, Indians had been building birchbark canoes for centuries. They began construction of a new canoe by cutting large sheets of bark from birch trees and laying them on the ground. The craftsmen worked in the shade to protect the bark from the sun.

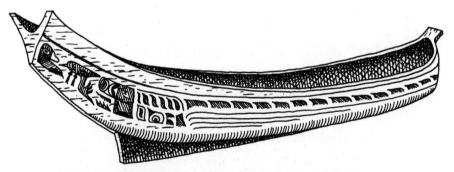

Haida canoes decorated with tribal emblems traveled the inlets and sounds of the Pacific Northwest.

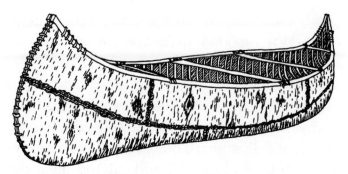

Refined by generations of craftsmen, the birchbark canoe was so well designed that it still serves as the model for most modern canoes.

Next, they constructed the frame of the canoe on top of the bark. Straight-grained lengths of cedar and ash were the materials of choice. The Indians carved, steamed, and bent the wood into ribs, thwarts, keels, and specially-shaped pieces for the stem and stern. They lashed the frame together with lengths of split spruce root. With care, they pulled the birch bark around the frame and stitched it in place with more root. Finally, they sealed the stitch holes and seams in the bark with boiled tree pitch.

You might think canoes made of bark would be fragile, but in fact they were remarkably sturdy. A bark canoe was sufficiently pliant to absorb the glancing impact of submerged rocks. If the bark was punctured by a sharp stone or torn by a snag, a canoeist could sew a patch in place, caulk it with sticky pitch, and continue on his way. With proper care, a birchbark canoe was good for many years of hard use before it began to deteriorate.

The birchbark canoe was so efficient and durable that it was the primary means of exploration and commerce on the wild waters of North America for decades. In Canada, the Hudson Bay Company depended upon bark canoes large enough to carry a dozen voyageurs and hundreds of pounds of supplies and furs.

The wilderness journeys of hardy voyageurs and explorers have made the birchbark canoe the stuff of legend. As Lewis and Clark embarked in 1803 on their great journey from St. Louis to the Pacific Ocean, Captain Lewis wrote in his journal:

> Our vessels consisted of six small canoes, and two large pirogues. This little fleet, although not quite so respectable as those of Columbus or Captain Cook, were still viewed by us with as much pleasure as those deservedly famed adventurers ever beheld theirs; and I daresay with quite as much anxiety for their safety and preservation. We were now about to penetrate a country at least two thousand miles in width, on which the foot of civilized man had never trodden; the good or evil it had in store for us was

for experiment yet to determine, and these little vessels contained every article by which we were to expect to subsist or defend ourselves.*

Over the years, bark suitable for making canoes became increasingly difficult to find, and the skill required to build a good bark canoe became even more rare. Thus it was not the birchbark canoe, but rather an ungainly vessel from England that first brought to the American public the idea of the canoe as a sporting craft rather than as a vessel for work.

The January 1876 edition of *The Canoeist*, an English journal, claims the first recorded cruise in a modern canoe (one made of materials other than bark or a hollow log) was undertaken by Sir Henry Debathe on the Thames River in a craft made of tin. That same year Scotsman John MacGregor launched a canoe that led to the first great canoeing fad.

An ardent adventurer and writer, MacGregor had come to America in 1859 and paddled in bark canoes, pirogues, and Eskimo kayaks. Upon his return to England, he modified the kayak design to make a canoe made of milled lumber. It had a covered deck and could accommodate a single

*G. Mercer Adam, *Makers of American History: The Lewis and Clark Exploring Expedition, 1804–06* (New York: The University Society, 1904), 40.

paddler using a double-bladed kayak paddle. MacGregor christened his craft the *Rob Roy* in honor of his ancestor Rob Roy MacGregor, made famous as a character in a novel by Sir Walter Scott.

In 1865, MacGregor embarked on a paddling tour of Europe. He wrote about his adventures in *A Thousand Miles in the Rob Roy Canoe on Twenty Rivers and Lakes of Europe*. The book sold briskly, and MacGregor was well received on the lecture circuits. The publicity he gave canoeing soon made it a very popular pastime in Great Britain.

As the sport spread, decked canoes like the *Rob Roy* sprouted masts for sails, keels for stability, and the sort of nautical hardware more commonly associated with sloops. The public began to perceive a canoe as a tiny sailboat, rigged for racing with the wind.

This was not just a poor man's yacht. The Royal Canoe Club, founded with MacGregor's help in 1866, included such notables as the Prince of Wales. Canoe sailors held regattas and devoted no small amount of capital and ingenuity to improving the speed and handling of their little ships.

Americans had their own adventurers who matched the feats of MacGregor in the *Rob Roy*. In 1874, Nathaniel Holmes Bishop paddled from Troy, New York, to Cedar Springs, Florida, in the *Maria Theresa*, a 15-foot canoe constructed of strips of thick manila paper glued over a frame. The total weight of the boat, paddler, gear, and provisions for the long cruise, said Bishop, "fell considerably short of the three Saratoga trunks containing a very modest wardrobe for a lady's four weeks' visit at a fashionable watering-place."

In 1885, dentist Charles Neide and a companion paddled and portaged a Rob Roy canoe from upper New York State to the Gulf of Mexico, a 3,300-mile journey. "My canoe had the roughest kind of usage," Neide reported in *Field & Stream.* "Heavily laden, she was portaged for seventy miles by rail and many more in a springless wagon over rough roads; was jumped over dams, tracked

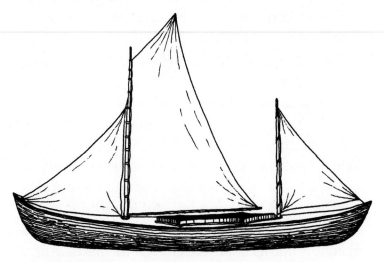

The exploits of explorers and the competition at canoe regattas thrust the decked canoe into prominence in the last third of the 19th century.

over the stony bed of the Allegheny River, banged against snags in the Mississippi, and dashed on the hard sand beaches of the Gulf of Mexico by the powerful force of the surf. I used her as a sleeping apartment for more than five months."

Paddling both birchbark and Rob Roy canoes, Willard Glazier traveled the full 3,184-mile length of the Mississippi River in 117 days. J. C. Haines paddled to the headwaters of the Columbia River in 1887 then back down the Kootenay River in British Columbia. In a letter to J. Henry Rushton, the maker of the canoe, he wrote:

> I have seen and portaged that which few white men have ever beheld and no map makers ever located, the Great Falls of the Kootenay, and am here to tell the tale, although had it not been for the thorough and honest workmanship displayed in the building of my canoe, I should now have been sleeping at their foot. I have jumped lesser falls, overcome huge whirlpools, run roaring mountain canyons and rapids without number; and have returned with the most thorough respect for the decked canoe that man can have for any creation of man.*

---

*Atwood Manley, *Rushton and His Time in American Canoeing* (Syracuse, New York: Syracuse University Press, 1968), 137–38.

15

A modern canoe is the result of centuries of innovation.

These and other exploits, along with the establishment of nearly 100 American canoe clubs and the staging of thousands of regattas, fueled American enthusiasm for canoeing. The very popularity of canoe clubs, however, held back the full realization of recreational canoeing. The focus of the clubs was nearly always on decked canoes rigged for sailing, and the regattas were frequently limited to sailors with decked boats. Many hobbyists found those tiny sailing craft too expensive and difficult to manage. Then, as the 1800s drew to a close, the bicycle craze swept across the country, and many would-be canoeists swapped their paddles for pedals.

At about the turn of the century, several New England boat makers began building open canoes of the traditional birchbark design, but with materials other than bark. They stretched tough canvas over a wooden frame and made it waterproof with layers of lacquer. Open canoes of good quality became readily available.

Since then, the history of canoeing has been a story of improved materials with only minor changes in the basic design. Whether made of canvas, aluminum, fiberglass, or some space-age plastic, today's canoes have a shape and structure very similar to those craft the Indians paddled out to meet the ships of European explorers.

When you paddle a canoe, you're not just riding in a boat. You've settled aboard a legend, a hint of the past, a link with hundreds of years of back-country travel. You are becoming part of a great, ongoing adventure.

Selecting a Canoe—
One Hour

A fine canoe is never the result of chance.

> —J. Henry Rushton,
> 19th century canoe maker

No matter how good this book is, reading alone won't teach you to paddle. To learn how to canoe in a day, you must have access to a canoe. I would like to have saved you the trouble of finding your own by attaching a complimentary canoe to each copy of this book, but since that was impossible, you'll have to get your own. It can be borrowed, rented, found abandoned on a beach, or liberated from the dust of a distant relative's musty basement. As long as it stays afloat and fulfills certain safety criteria, almost any canoe will serve you well enough at first. You can get a feel for what it's like to be on the water, to handle a paddle, and to gain control over a canoe.

Most importantly, you'll develop a sense of what you like and dislike about a certain canoe. Later, when you're in a position to select from among several canoes to lease or buy, you'll have some experience upon which to base your decision.

For even that first outing, a bit of knowledge about canoes will make your day on the water more enjoyable. If you can identify the parts of a canoe, you'll know where to examine one in order to determine if it is seaworthy. You can converse intelligently about canoes with salespeople and paddling companions. You can impress your friends when conversation turns to the finer points of canoe construction. Canoe purists, incidentally, never refer to their craft as "boats."

Parts of a Canoe

Bow and Stern

The front of a canoe is the *bow*, and the back is the *stern*. To discern the difference, notice the placement of the seats. The back seat will be closer to the stern than the front seat is to the bow.

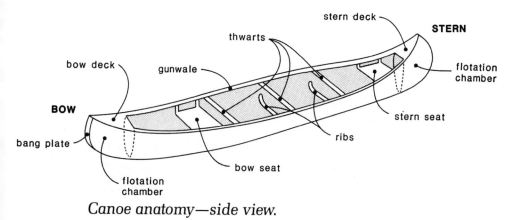

Canoe anatomy—side view.

They're set that way to give the person in each seat as much legroom as possible.

Occasionally you may find a canoe with a single seat mounted near the center. Designed for a solo paddler, that canoe is also probably shorter and narrower than two-seated models. Again, consider the legroom; the solo seat will be a little further from the bow than it is from the stern.

Bang Plate

The bows and sterns of canoes are often shielded with wooden or metal strips called *bang plates*. They serve a purpose similar to bumpers on automobiles. Like most modern-day bumpers, bang plates are meant to absorb only the stress of low-speed impact. It's best to treat your canoe as if the bow and stern had no protection at all, and avoid collisions with the shore, docks, and other canoes.

Gunwales

The "railings" extending from the bow to the stern along the tops of the sides of a canoe are the *gunwales* (pronounced "GUN-els"). They lend structural stability to the craft and give you something to grab when you require some additional stability yourself.

Thwarts

Thwarts are the crosspieces spanning the canoe from one gunwale to the other. Generally, you'll find one to four thwarts, depending upon the length and material of the canoe. Like the gunwales, thwarts increase a canoe's rigidity and strength. Most are not designed to support heavy weight placed directly upon them, which is a polite way of saying don't sit on the thwarts.

Ribs

Attached to both gunwales and curving down the sides and across the bottom, *ribs* help give the canoe its basic configuration. In the birchbark canoes of old, wooden ribs forced into place after the bark had been sewn to the gunwales pushed the skin of the canoe into a taut, smooth shape.

Wooden ribs are still used in canvas-covered canoes and in some fiberglass models. Aluminum canoes have metal ribs that serve both as stiffeners and as braces to which the aluminum sheeting is riveted. Some canoes made of space-age materials are sufficiently stiff to eliminate the need for ribs.

Deck

Many canoes have a small *deck* covering the first foot or two behind the bow, and another just forward of the stern. These decks often top off sealed compartments filled with foam to provide extra flotation.

Keel

The *keel* is a band of metal or wood on the bottom of the canoe. Running from bow to stern, it stiffens the canoe and shields it from scrapes against underwater obstacles. Extending a little below the craft like a fin, the keel also helps keep a canoe on a straight course.

Canoe Size and Shape

Paddlers can select from a wide range of sizes and shapes of canoes and materials of construc-

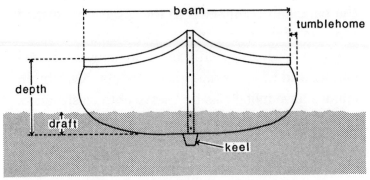

Canoe anatomy—front view.

tion. Each variation has some effect upon the handling qualities of a craft in different types of water, and upon its weight, capacity, and ease of maintenance.

Length

From bow to stern, modern canoes measure from 14 to 20 feet. A craft of about 16 to 18 feet is a good size for two paddlers. Longer canoes can carry more weight, but can also be more difficult to manage in the water and heavier to portage. Shorter canoes work well for solo paddlers but may not have the legroom needed by a crew of two.

Beam

The width of a canoe at its widest point is its *beam*. The greater its beam, the more stable a canoe will be. General-use canoes have a beam of about 36 inches.

Depth

The vertical distance of the side of a canoe as measured from the lowest point of the gunwale to keel level is the craft's *depth*. The greater the depth, the less the likelihood water will splash over the side. A canoe with exceptional depth can haul massive loads before the weight lowers the gunwales too near the water. On the other hand, increased depth adds weight to a canoe. High sides can also catch crosswinds, making it more difficult to steer.

Chines and Tumblehome

Chines and *tumblehome* are terms so pleasant to pronounce that you'll want to know them if only for the joy of rolling the words off your tongue.

Look straight down the side of a canoe. The rounded, puffed-cheek shape of the wall of a craft is its *tumblehome*. A canoe with a large tumblehome can be more stable than one with straighter sides; however, paddlers in that more forgiving canoe will have to reach out a little further with each stroke of their paddles.

The chines of a canoe are the concave interiors of the craft's sides—essentially the inside of the tumblehome. Solo canoeists sitting near the center of their canoes sometimes brace themselves by tucking one leg against the chine.

Materials

The material from which a canoe is constructed helps determine the strength, durability, and sometimes the handling qualities of the craft. Your choices will probably fall among one of the following.

Wood

A close link to the craft of a century ago, wooden canoes are still made today. They are often given the careful construction and finish of fine furniture, and the completed canoe is as much a work of art as it is a watercraft. The most traditional models are made completely of wood, or feature an outer skin of lacquered canvas. Some makers incorporate fiberglass, resins, and other modern materials into traditional wood designs.

A wood or wood and canvas canoe is a good choice for a paddler who takes pleasure in using a quality craft and in lavishing loving care on it when it is out of the water. These canoes require occasional maintenance to keep them in top condition. Abraded canvas needs to be repaired. The wood may require sanding and refinishing.

Aluminum

The widespread use of metal in canoes came as an outgrowth of the aircraft industry. After World War II, companies that had been building fighters and bombers sought to diversify their product lines. An aluminum canoe, with its long, curved shape and strut-like thwarts and ribs, is similar in construction to the fuselage of an airplane.

Aluminum is light, sturdy, and easy to shape. Foam-filled flotation chambers in the bow and stern of a metal canoe make it unsinkable. On all but the wildest rivers, such a canoe is virtually indestructible. Since there is nothing that will rot or rust, aluminum craft require little maintenance.

The drawbacks of aluminum canoes are primarily aesthetic. They are noisy. The sound of a paddle banging against a metal gunwale echoes across the water with a dissonance alien to any natural setting. In texture and appearance, aluminum is far from birchbark or even green canvas. If that doesn't bother you, you're all set. If it does, you may find the canoe of your dreams made of a space-age material.

Fiberglass

Canoe makers moving beyond aluminum found fiberglass suitable for their needs. It is tough, molds well, and lasts a long time. Building with fiberglass, however, requires a high degree of skill. Canoes made of the material vary greatly in quality and weight.

ABS, Kevlar

ABS (marketed under various trade names such as Royalex), Kevlar, and other space-age materials are very tough and have some of the satisfying give not possible in more rigid aluminum craft. They stand up to the elements better than fiberglass and also are lighter. Constructed with wooden thwarts and gunwales, they can approach the aesthetic appeal of wood and canvas canoes.

Inflatable Canoes

Inflatable canoes are hybrids—the fat offspring of canoes, kayaks, and truck tire inner tubes. Some are rugged enough for hard use. Others are little more than giant bathtub toys.

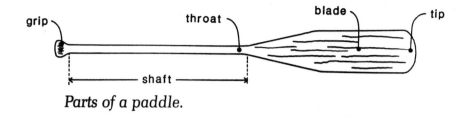

Parts of a paddle.

The techniques you use to paddle a real canoe will also lend themselves to propelling an inflatable, but the air-filled versions will be very sluggish in comparison to their sleek counterparts. Switch to an inflatable after some time in a good canoe, and you'll think you're paddling your way through a pond of molasses.

Paddles

There was a time when all canoe paddles were carved of clear, straight-grained ash, maple, spruce, or pine, but just as modern materials have changed the composition of canoes, so plastic and metal have given manufacturers new options for making paddles.

A plastic grip and blade riveted to an aluminum shaft creates a long-lasting paddle that is as light and tough as its wooden counterparts. What it lacks, though, is the same spirit missing in metal canoes. A wooden paddle, like a handcrafted canoe, feels right. It ages well. Best of all, it is virtually identical to the paddles of old. While that can be a more symbolic gesture than a choice of cold reason, you may find these considerations important.

The length of the paddle best for you depends upon your height. For starters, select one that reaches from the floor to somewhere between the middle of your chest and your nose. After you've done a bit of canoeing, you may find that a shorter or longer paddle is more appropriate for your paddling style and the type of canoeing you do most.

Weight is also a factor. You'll be lifting your paddle hundreds of times a day on the water. If everything else is equal, choose a light paddle over a heavy one.

Life Jackets

A personal flotation device (PFD) is an absolute necessity for every person setting out in a canoe. A life jacket will keep you afloat if you fall overboard or your canoe capsizes. A PFD will hold your head above the water and allow you to breathe, even if you are unconscious.

A life jacket is the most inexpensive and most effective form of life insurance available. Be sure everyone in your canoe has one and wears it.

Bailer

While you are paddling, it's not unusual for some water to splash into your canoe. With a bailer on board, you can keep your canoe relatively dry. Make one from an empty one-gallon plastic jug.

Wear a life jacket (PFD) whenever you are on the water.

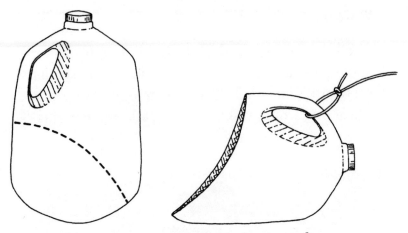

Cut off the bottom of a plastic jug to make a bailer.

Without removing the handle or the lid, cut the jug as shown in the accompanying illustration. Use the bailer to scoop puddles and pools from the canoe floor. To prevent the bailer from floating away, tie one end of a 10-foot length of cord to its handle and the other end to a thwart of your canoe.

A sponge is handy too, for wiping up paddle drip.

Painter

Painter is a nautical term for a line used to secure a boat. Many canoes have a metal loop riveted to the bang plate. A 25-foot line of $3/8$- to $1/2$-inch nylon cord tied to the loop or to a thwart will come in handy when you are tying up to a dock or pulling your canoe through shallow water. When you're not using the line, keep it out of the way by coiling it and tying the coil to a thwart or taping it down with duct tape.

Clothing

When you're canoeing, the sun's rays can be brutal. They'll hit you on their way down and smack you again as they ricochet off the surface of the water. Use plenty of effective sunscreen. If you're especially sensitive to the sun, put on a broad-brimmed hat and wear a lightweight, long-sleeve shirt and long pants. Wear sunglasses.

Of greater immediate concern is the potential for becoming chilled. Should your clothing get wet on a cool, windy day, you may find yourself shivering far from shore, even in mild weather. There's a real danger of hypothermia—becoming so chilled your body has difficulty re-warming itself. Always take along the clothing you need to prevent hypothermia. Include a warm Windbreaker or jacket, and perhaps a wool shirt or sweater.

On some days you shouldn't go canoeing. If a storm is brewing, especially one that could produce lightning, stay home. Paddling in frosty weather or on cold water is possible if you wear a wet suit like those favored by kayakers and skin divers. Otherwise, the risk of hypothermia is simply too great.

Finally, take along a swimsuit and towel, and wear shoes you won't mind getting wet. Old tennis shoes or canvas boating shoes are ideal. Your footwear should provide good traction and protect your feet from underwater rocks, but not be so heavy and bulky as to weigh you down or scuff the inside of your canoe.

Lunch

Paddling burns up a lot of calories. As you learn how to canoe in one day, you'll get hungry before you get home. Pack some sandwiches, fruit, and a bottle of water. I like to include a handful of freshly baked chocolate chip cookies.

Carrying Clothing and Gear

Pack food, extra clothing, equipment, and other items in a plastic trash bag to keep them dry. Twist the top closed, tie it with a cord, and knot one end of the cord around a thwart to prevent the bag from drifting away if you capsize.

Moving onto the Water—Two Hours

You'll want to find a quiet lake or pond for your first outing in a canoe. Almost any body of still water will do. If there's a sloping beach leading into the water, so much the better. City, state, and federal parks often allow canoes on their waters. Check on specific regulations by calling their offices of recreation. While you're learning the basics, it's best to avoid streams and rivers. You'll have enough to think about without concerns that a strong current may carry you downstream.

Bodies of water are sometimes controlled with man-made structures which can cause dangerous *hydraulics*. Water going over even a very low dam can churn back upon itself, creating a suction at the base of the dam that can trap boaters and

Hydraulics are dangerous roils created by water rushing over dams, sluiceways, and other diversions. The suction they cause can capsize and trap an unwary canoeist.

swimmers. The only sure way to deal safely with dams, sluiceways, millraces, and the like is to stay well clear of them.

If you do venture onto a stream or river, take care to avoid strainers and rapids—natural hazards that can be deadly to a canoeist just learning to paddle. *Strainers* are branches of trees that hang down into the water. A canoe drifting into a strainer may be snagged by the branches and capsize as the current continues to push the craft forward. Canoeists tangled in strainers can find it difficult to break free.

Rapids are a novice paddler's nightmare and an experienced canoeist's dream. Mastering the art of reading and navigating a stream rushing among boulders and dropping over underwater ledges requires a serious commitment to learn from people who know what they are doing. As a beginning canoeist, it's best to treat rapids just as you do hydraulics and strainers—simply don't go there.

Stay clear of branches dragging in the water. Known as strainers, they can entangle and flip a canoe.

Even the most seasoned paddlers get knowledgeable information about rivers before they put their canoes in the water. Should you find yourself in a current carrying you toward a stretch of water with which you are unfamiliar, pull into shore. Secure your canoe, then walk downstream until you can judge the conditions ahead. Don't drift blindly into water you may not be able to manage.

Two people can lift a canoe to a roof rack.

Moving a Canoe on Land

A canoe on dry land is an ungainly beast. Lifting, carrying, and launching a canoe require some care, leverage, and good fortune. At first, the process also requires two people.

Canoes are usually stored keel up on the ground or a rack. To get one up and moving, station yourself and a partner at opposite ends. Bend your knees and grasp the bow while your partner does the same at the stern. Lift with your legs rather than your back, and turn the canoe upright. Take care not to drop the canoe; the impact can crack its ribs, pop the rivets, or damage it in some other way. Grasp the righted canoe firmly by the bow and stern decks, and you're ready to carry it short distances.

Roof Racks

If your canoe is stored a long way from where you intend to go, you may need to carry it on a roof rack on your vehicle. Watercraft rental centers usually can provide you with a rack when you pick up a canoe. Roof racks designed to carry bicycles, kayaks, and general cargo usually lend themselves to toting canoes as well. Follow the instructions for mounting the rack on your car; most clamp onto the gutters above the doors. Make sure it is

Center the canoe on the roof rack and tie securely.

solidly attached. If the car has a radio antenna, lower it.

To put a canoe on a rack, begin by placing it parallel to the automobile, with one person at the bow and the other at the stern. Facing one another, grasp the canoe deck with the hand closest to the car. Place the other hand under the keel.

With a smooth motion, lift the canoe as you straighten your legs, then rotate it toward the car and slide it upside down onto the roof rack. Scoot the canoe forward or backward until it is centered over the car and secure it to the rack with strong line or straps. A 50-foot length of ½-inch nylon rope works well. Next, attach a 25-foot length of

Secure the ends of the canoe to the car's bumpers or frame.

*Pick up your canoe at each end and carry it to
the water.*

line to the bow and another to the stern, then loop
them around the car's bumpers and tie down.

Get behind the wheel and be sure you have ade-
quate visibility for safe driving. Don't forget the
life jackets, paddles, and other gear. Once you hit
the road, stop after a few miles to check your
knots.

Remove a canoe from a car-top rack by reversing the steps you used to get it there. Be especially careful not to drop the canoe as you lower it to the ground.

Launching

Now the real fun begins. Pull on your swimsuit, shoes, and life jacket, then carry your canoe to the edge of the lake and place it on the ground. Prop a paddle inside the canoe beside each seat. Tie the bailer to a thwart and the painter to a thwart or bang plate loop.

A canoe is designed to be very strong while it is on the water. It is not built to be dragged across the ground, run into the shore, or left propped half in and half out of the water. Protect your canoe from that sort of unwarranted abuse by making one small sacrifice—wet feet. Working with a partner, lift the canoe by the bow and stern decks and walk into the water until it is deep enough to float your craft.

Once the canoe is floating, the person near the stern can steady it while the other steps aboard and gets situated in the bow seat, paddle in hand. That done, the stern paddler, holding the gunwales for support, steps into the back and takes the stern seat.

Launching a canoe. Wet feet and canoeing often go together.

To launch from a low dock, the two of you can stand amidships on either side of the canoe and face each other. Lift the canoe by the gunwales, tilt it until the bow touches the water, then pass the canoe hand-over-hand onto the lake. Tie the free end of the painter to the dock.

As you step into the canoe, keep your weight centered over the keel and hold the gunwales for

Paddle away from shore. Wear a life jacket when-
ever you are on the water.

support until you're seated. Climb in one at a time. Whoever is not moving can help steady the craft.

Paddle away from shore into water that's about chest deep. (You can measure it by feeling for the bottom with your paddle.) It won't be difficult to imagine the adventures that lie ahead, but before you go any farther, you should capsize your canoe.

Rock your canoe from side to side until it capsizes. Try to hang on to a gunwale as the craft goes over.

Capsizing

Learning to canoe by capsizing may seem a little like mastering the automobile by driving into a tree. An intentional dunking, however, will help you become familiar with the limits of your canoe and allow you to practice what to do if you ever accidentally flip.

Lean far to one side. Lean back the other way. Holding the gunwales for support, bounce up and down in your seat. As the craft fights to stay upright, you may be surprised at how difficult it is to overturn a canoe. However if you lean far enough, water will flood over a gunwale and the canoe will swamp.

Unintentional capsizing is most often the result of sudden, unexpected, or exaggerated movement of paddlers. The one rule to remember when a canoe capsizes is this: STAY WITH THE CANOE! The reason is simple: A CANOE WILL NOT SINK!

A flooded canoe may ride very low in the water, but it will never dive to the bottom. All canoes possess a natural buoyancy that keeps them on the surface. Flotation chambers in the bows and sterns of aluminum canoes prevent them from going down.

Maintain contact with your canoe and you won't sink, either. As the canoe is overturning, try to keep your eye on it, and keep a hand on the gunwale. If you're thrown clear, get back to the canoe as quickly as you can and hang on to the gunwale.

Think of a flooded canoe as a giant flotation device. Get back into your canoe and you'll be more comfortable than you are bobbing around in the water. You can also paddle a swamped canoe to the beach.

A canoe full of water tends to float right side up. If yours is upside down, pull on the keel or on the bow and stern to flip it over. That done, move to the middle of the canoe where the sides are lowest so you and your partner can get back on board.

A flooded canoe is buoyant enough to keep you above water.

This is easy to do if you hoist your upper body over the gunwale, then support your weight with your hands on the floor while you swing your legs inside. Increase the canoe's stability by sitting on the floor rather than the seats. Even with the addition of your weight and your partner's, the canoe will stay afloat.

Your paddles might drift away while you're scrambling aboard. Use your hands as oars to propel your flooded canoe close enough to the paddles to retrieve them, then use the paddles to make your way ashore.

Once in the shallows, hop out, grasp the canoe by the bow and stern, and empty it by rolling it sideways as you lift it clear of the lake.

You may want to repeat the capsizing drill a few times, especially if the day is hot and the water is particularly inviting. Try standing up in your canoe before it goes over. Switch places with your partner, bounce up and down, and rock the canoe from side to side. You'll soon develop a solid trust in your canoe, and will instinctively remember to hang onto it any time it does capsize.

Paddling—Two Hours

Once you get a feel for the strokes described in this chapter, paddling a canoe across still water will be easy. Granted, canoeing is an art, and there are people who spend years mastering its finer points. Nevertheless, a few hours practicing the most important strokes will give you the skill and confidence you need to be comfortable on the water, and inspire you to become the best canoeist you can.

Paddling

With the help of your partner, launch your canoe. This is a good time to practice pushing off. To launch from a beach, the stern paddler stands at the edge of the water and holds the canoe steady while the bow paddler climbs aboard and gets situated in the front seat. The stern paddler steps into the craft and pushes the canoe away from shore with a free foot before settling into the rear seat.

The birchbark canoes of old seldom had seats, a pattern followed by many canoe makers into the early decades of this century. Paddlers positioned themselves by kneeling in the bottom of their craft. You may want to do this sometimes, too. If waves begin rocking your canoe or you see the wake of a speedboat rolling toward you, dropping your weight low in the canoe will greatly increase its stability.

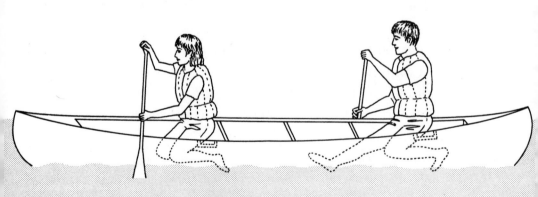

Paddlers may kneel on the floor of a canoe or take a seat and stretch out one or both legs.

For comfort, perch yourself on a canoe seat.

For more stability, kneel in the bottom of the canoe.

Most people, however, find it uncomfortable to kneel or sit on their heels for long periods of time. Nearly all modern canoes come equipped with seats that allow you to stretch out your legs or extend one leg and tuck the other back underneath.

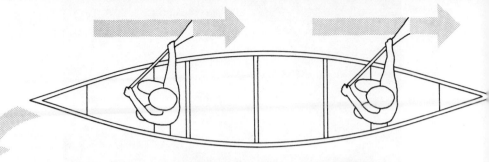

A forward or power stroke moves a canoe ahead and causes it to turn *away* from the paddles.

Begin the forward stroke by dipping most of the blade into the water ahead of you.

Forward Stroke

The forward stroke does just what you would expect—it moves the canoe ahead. Because it can

Continue the forward stroke by drawing the paddle blade alongside your craft. Use the muscles of your shoulders as well as those of your arms.

make your canoe leap across the water, some canoeists call it the *power stroke*. Here's how it's done.

Hold the paddle with one hand on the throat and the other on the grip (see illustration of paddle parts). Lean forward, dip most of the blade into the water, and draw the paddle alongside the canoe.

As the paddle comes out of the water, make a smooth *recovery* by swinging it forward and dipping it back into the water. During the recovery, you can twist your wrists a little to turn the blade parallel to the surface of the water. Called *feathering*, it allows the paddle to cut through the air without slowing your forward progress.

Why Canoes Go in Circles

As you keep paddling with the forward stroke, you'll soon notice that although the canoe is moving, it's not necessarily going where you want it to go. If the person in either the bow or stern seat paddles alone on the right side of the canoe, it will turn left. Paddle on the left side and the canoe will curve to the right. Paddle long enough on one side and you'll go in a circle.

What you're dealing with here is the undeniable tenet of Newtonian physics, which states that every action has an opposite and equal reaction. Pressure exerted by a paddle against the water causes the canoe to move away from the blade. Most of the force of a paddle stroke is directed backward, so the canoe glides ahead. But since the paddle is moving on one side of the canoe rather than in a direct line with the keel, the canoe will also slide sideways with each stroke.

You can overcome this circling problem by taking a few strokes on one side, then stroking several times on the other side. By shifting back and forth, you can hold a fairly steady course.

When both of you paddle on the same side at the same time, the canoe, of course, turns more quickly than if you paddle on opposite sides. The stern paddler's strokes have a stronger effect on the direction of a canoe than do the bow paddler's efforts. Because of this, the canoeist in the stern is captain of this tiny ship and can usually do the most to influence its direction of travel.

The bow paddler sets the pace of the strokes for the person in the stern to match. And since the bow paddler has a better view of the water immediately ahead, it is well within nautical tradition for him to shout timely observations such as,

The stern paddler can influence the direction of a canoe more than a paddler in the bow. As paddlers lay down forward strokes on opposite sides of the canoe, the craft still turns away from the paddle of the person in the back.

"We're not really going to run into that rock, are we?"

As you string together a series of forward strokes, maintain a rhythmic, easy motion. You don't need to muscle the paddle through quiet water. A fluid dip and swing of the blade will take you where you want to go and conserve your energies through the day. A light hand on the paddle is much better than wrestling a canoe from place to place.

Switching your paddles from one side to the other in order to maintain a course is all right for a while, but it is awkward and ungainly, especially when there is a much more effective and graceful alternative—the forward stroke with steering corrections.

Forward Stroke with Steering Corrections

Think of the rudder on a sailing ship. When the rudder is turned to the right, the flow of onrushing water presses against it, pushing the stern away from the flow and causing the ship itself to bear to the right. Likewise, a rudder turned the other way will swing a ship to the left.

You can use your paddle to steer your canoe in much the same way as a ship uses its rudder. Instruct the bow paddler to use a simple forward

The rudder move. At the end of a forward stroke, turn the blade of the paddle parallel with the water and angle it into the flow of water.

stroke on the left side of the canoe. Sitting in the stern, you'll employ the forward stroke on the right side. As the canoe picks up speed, it will begin turning to the left.

To bring the canoe back on course, keep your paddle in the water at the end of a forward stroke and twist your left wrist toward your chin so the paddle blade is turned parallel with the canoe, transforming your paddle into a rudder.

Now pull your left hand toward you, angling the blade away from the canoe. Use your right hand on the throat of the paddle as a fulcrum. You'll feel the force of the water pushing against the paddle, and the canoe will swing back into line. Lift the paddle out of the water and make a recovery just as you would at the end of an ordinary forward stroke.

Paddle a few more times to bring your canoe back up to speed, then repeat the rudder move to correct your course. Try holding the blade at different angles and notice how that changes the effectiveness of the maneuver.

After you gain some confidence using the rudder move on the right side of the canoe, try it on the left. The bow paddler will need to switch to the right side and continue laying down forward strokes.

The difficulties you may encounter are these:

- Not turning the paddle blade to the correct position to act as a rudder. Look down at the blade as you begin the rudder move. You should see just the top edge of the blade rather than the flat face.
- Despite holding the paddle in perfect rudder position, nothing happens. The canoe is probably moving too slowly. There must be a flow

of water against the paddle blade for it to do its work. Unless your canoe is traveling fast enough to wander off course, a rudder move is neither necessary nor possible.

- Losing too much speed while using a rudder move. The pressure of water that shoves against the blade and begins a turn also creates drag that slows your canoe. While a small rudder move results in a gradual change in direction, a sharp pull on the paddle may bring the canoe to a halt rather than creating the expected sweeping change in direction. A series of three or four forward strokes with small rudder moves is usually more effective in making a large turn than is a single stroke and rudder.

- Squashing the thumb of your fulcrum hand between the throat of the paddle and the canoe. Try using the gunwale itself as the fulcrum. Brace the throat against the gunwale rather than your hand. Pull the grip toward your chest, and the canoe will turn.

After you've practiced the steering stroke for a while, put into shore and trade places with the bow paddler. That way, each of you will have a chance to steer the canoe from the stern. Using the paddle as a rudder, you should be able to land wherever you want.

Before you push off again, stand on dry land for a few minutes and practice the forward stroke and rudder move in the air. Watch the movement of the paddle, and you may develop a better sense of the position in which to hold the blade.

Steering Stroke

Until now, you've been working with two distinct actions. The forward stroke gives your canoe momentum; the rudder move holds it on course.

Now blend the two actions into one smooth motion. Start by making a good forward stroke. As you come to the end of the stroke, twist the paddle grip toward you to put the blade in the rudder position. For just a moment, angle the blade into the flow of the water to return the canoe to its course. Finish by lifting your paddle from the water and swinging it forward to start the next stroke.

Combining the forward stroke and rudder move in one continuous, rhythmic motion creates the steering stroke. That small bit of rudder action at the end of each pass of the paddle counteracts the turning power of the forward stroke and keeps the canoe going straight.

Master the forward stroke and steering stroke, and you'll know as much about paddling on still water as most canoeists. Then learn the following five strokes for special maneuvers, and you'll be well on your way to becoming an accomplished canoeist.

The secret to the steering stroke is a quick rudder move just before the paddle comes out of the water.

Rudder Turn

With the steering stroke, you saw how the person in the stern holds the paddle in rudder position at the end of each stroke. A little rudder with each stroke was enough to make the canoe run straight.

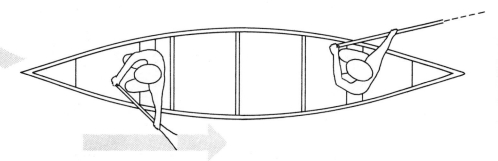

Holding the paddle like a rudder turns the canoe to the right.

Now try using the rudder sharply. Make a forward stroke, turn the paddle to rudder position, then pull the grip well in toward your chest so that the blade extends away from the canoe at a 45-degree angle. If the craft is traveling at good speed, it will turn sharply to the right; use the rudder on the left, and the bow will turn hard to the left.

The rudder turn is important if you must swerve quickly to miss a stump or submerged rock, or if you suddenly realize you've left your lunch on shore and need to swing around to pick it up. Like the rudder stroke, the rudder turn is only effective when done by the stern paddler. The bow paddler may use the sweep or draw strokes (explained below) to help swing the canoe onto its new course.

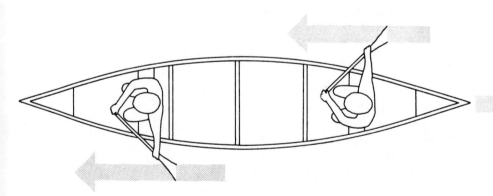

In the back stroke, the paddles go forward and force the canoe to travel in reverse.

Back Stroke

The back stroke is simply the forward stroke in reverse. As a result, the canoe moves backward.

Use the back stroke to extricate your canoe from tight spots, maneuver it around obstacles, parallel park next to a dock and, most important, bring it to a quick stop. Think of the back stroke as the brakes on your canoe. No matter how fast the craft is moving, if both paddlers hit still water with several strong back strokes, the canoe will come to a dead stop. A few more strokes and it will reverse its direction.

Sweep Stroke

A simple forward stroke on the right side of a canoe will turn it gradually to the left. A *sweep stroke* is a sort of supercharged forward stroke that will turn the canoe much more quickly. It is most often used by the bow paddler, as in the accompanying drawing. When the bow and stern paddlers are both paddling on the same side of the canoe, however, the sweep stroke can be very effective for sharp turns.

Instead of pulling the blade through the water close alongside the canoe as you would with a forward stroke, sweep the submerged blade in an arc at arm's length from the canoe. For the front

In a sweep stroke, the blade of the paddle describes an arc alongside the canoe.

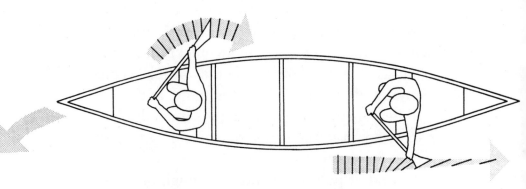

A bow paddler can use the sweep stroke to make a canoe turn sharply. In this case, the steering stroke of the stern paddler also helps.

paddler, the first half of the arc pushes away the bow, causing the canoe to turn. For the paddler in the back, the second half of the sweeping arc pulls the stern toward the paddle, exaggerating the turning motion of the bow.

Draw Stroke

While the direction a canoe travels is usually determined by the stern paddler, the draw stroke allows the bow paddler to make quick course ad-

Begin a draw stroke by reaching out as far as you can and driving the paddle blade into the water.

Complete the draw stroke by pulling the paddle toward your canoe.

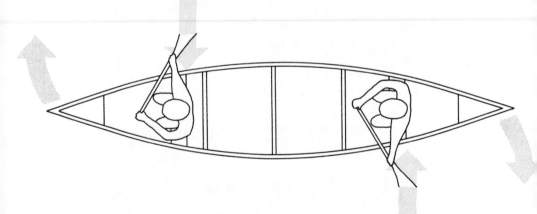

Digging their blades into the water and pulling the paddles close to the craft, paddlers draw the canoe in the direction they want it to go.

justments with or without the help of the stern paddler. Three or four fast, strong draw strokes can pull your canoe away from a rock, stump, or other obstacle. The stern paddler may also use a draw stroke to pull the stern of the canoe toward a beach or close to another canoe.

Begin a draw stroke by twisting your shoulders around, leaning over the gunwale, and digging the paddle into the water as far out to the side of the canoe as you can reach. Pull the face of the paddle toward you. As you do, you'll *draw* the canoe toward the blade. Recover the paddle and repeat the stroke.

Pry Stroke

Think of the pry stroke as the opposite of the draw. Hold the blade parallel to the canoe, dig it into the water close to the side, then push the blade out away from you. The canoe will respond by moving in the opposite direction of the paddle.

For more power on the pry stroke, use the gunwale as a fulcrum. Dip the blade into the water against the canoe. Pull back on the grip, letting the throat of the paddle rock against the gunwale as the blade is forced outward.

To move a canoe sideways toward a dock, both bow and stern paddlers can use the draw or pry strokes. To spin a craft around, the stern paddler

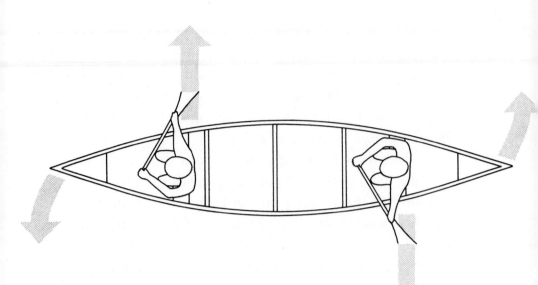

The pry of the pry stroke shoves the canoe away from the outward thrust of the paddles.

can use a pry stroke on one side while the bow paddler puts draw strokes on the other side. These strokes are especially important to whitewater canoeists because they give paddlers great steering control. If you master them while paddling on quiet lakes, you'll be able to use them easily to maneuver in faster water.

Solo Canoeing—
One Hour

There comes a day in every canoeing team's relationship when one of you can't or won't take to the water. Other plans have been made. The bathroom plumbing has rebelled. The in-laws are coming to visit. It's threatening to rain, is raining, has just rained.

Of course, the one who *does* want to go canoeing will see these as minor complications. Surely the bathroom repairs can wait a little longer. So, for that matter, can the relatives. And why should a little dampness stand in the way of sending a canoe gliding over the lake?

This time, however, your partner is adamant in refusing to join you. There are suggestions you might stay and help with the house, the plumbing, and the entertaining. You are tempted, but the lure of open water possesses the more magnetic attraction. Before long you're out the door and down at the water's edge.

You'll soon discover that apart from the lack of social pleasures, paddling alone is essentially the same as it is for a team. There are, however, a few crucial differences, which this chapter will address.

First, safety becomes an even more serious consideration for a solo paddler. Since no one may be around to come to your aid if you run into difficulty, you must take full responsibility for your own well-being. That means *always* wearing a life jacket. It means keeping a close eye on the weather and coming ashore at the first sign of stormy conditions.

As you learn how to canoe in one day, take an hour to try out the basics of solo canoeing. It's a good idea to have your partner on shore or in another canoe to shout encouragement and to help out if something goes awry.

Begin by launching your canoe and taking the stern position. Paddle away from shore with a good, strong steering stroke, the same you would use if you were the stern paddler of a team. Because you don't have a bow paddler offsetting the turning power of your own strokes, your canoe is more likely to swing to the side opposite that on which you're paddling. The bow of your canoe

A solo paddler can sit or kneel facing what is normally the rear of a two-seated canoe. Because this position is close to the center of the craft, it is ideal for effective paddling.

will ride higher on the water, where it can be easily blown off course by the wind. You'll need to use a more exaggerated version of the steering stroke to keep your canoe going straight. The most effective solution to this difficulty is also the most obvious: move closer to the center of the canoe.

Unfortunately, most canoes with two seats don't provide a very good place for you to perch in the middle. You don't want to sit on the center thwart. That can be hard on the canoe, and it puts you too far forward to paddle well.

Instead, try this little trick. Step past the center of the canoe then turn around so you are facing the stern. Kneel on one knee with your weight against the back edge of the bow seat or, if there is one, against the thwart. You may even be able to sit comfortably in the bow seat and face the stern. In all cases, the stern of your canoe is now the bow. Your weight is nearly amidships, which keeps the bow down in the water. You are in a perfect paddling position.

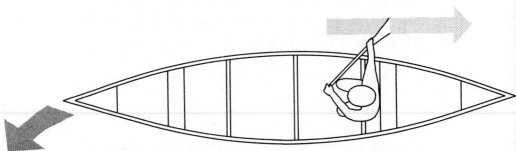

A solo paddler relying only on forward strokes will find the bow turning in the direction opposite the paddle.

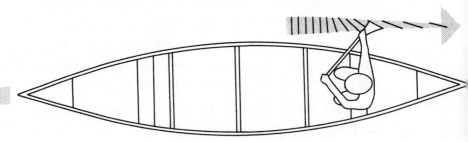

Using a steering stroke holds the canoe on a straight line.

Start out by paddling with the steering stroke. The first thing you'll probably notice is that since you're kneeling at about the widest part of the canoe, you have to lean out farther in order to dip your paddle into the water. Try sliding over against the side of the canoe on which you'll make your strokes so you won't have so far to reach. Of course, this will cause the canoe to list to the left, but that can be an advantage in several ways.

As you now know, a canoe has a natural tendency to turn away from the side on which you're paddling. A tilted canoe, however, tends to curve *the other way*—in the direction it is listing. By heeling your canoe to one side, you give yourself plenty of clearance to swing your paddle through each stroke. At the same time, you're putting the canoe in an attitude that helps it track a straight line.

Finally, a canoe listing to one side has less surface touching the water than one that's square with the world. Less surface means reduced friction and greater forward motion with each stroke.

Slide to the other side of the canoe, and you'll have all the room you need to make another series of strong steering strokes. The listing of the canoe will help counteract the turning force of your strokes.

Once you've become comfortable with these basics of solo paddling, you can modify your sitting position to increase your leverage and com-

By sliding to one side of the canoe, a solo paddler increases the efficiency of his strokes.

fort. For paddling on the left side, place your left knee in the bottom of the canoe and stretch your right leg out in front of you. Your left thigh will be against the side of the canoe, and your buttocks should be resting lightly against the edge of the seat or thwart.

Often used by solo canoe racers, this position can tilt the canoe so far that the gunwale may be only a few inches above the waterline. Braced against the seat or thwart and the floor and side of the canoe, you're in a good, stable position to throw your shoulders and back into your strokes.

If all this sliding and leaning feels awkward and complicated, forget it. Stay centered right over the keel and you can still paddle perfectly well, employing the same strokes as you would paddling from the stern seat.

Landing and Portaging—One Hour

I was 16 when I took my first canoe trip. For two weeks the members of my Boy Scout troop skimmed across the wide lakes of the Boundary Waters of northern Minnesota and southern Ontario. Each afternoon we pitched our tents on the wooded shores and built fires over which we broiled slabs of the northern pike we'd caught during the day.

We weren't very good canoeists at first. We capsized one canoe, drowned our toilet paper, and watched our cook pots float away. Although we were never completely lost, we experienced extended episodes of what a kind observer might call advanced spacial confusion.

Our paddling improved day by day, however. Even if we didn't always know quite where we were going, we became adept at keeping our little fleet traveling over the lakes. We no longer fell overboard. The surviving toilet paper was safe.

Our increasing skill at moving over the water did not extend to smooth overland travel. We could beach our canoes well enough, stepping out and into shallow water before the bows could grind into the gravel. We could even unload the big Duluth packs full of food and gear and send them with the first wave of Scouts up the portage trail toward the next lake. But what caused no end of difficulty was lifting the canoes out of the water and carrying them through the forest.

Our guide was a man of many seasons in the wild who had probably never suffered so much as he did watching us learn to canoe. As he paddled up to a portage, he would step lightly into the shallows and slip on his pack. Next, he would grasp his canoe by the gunwales and pull it up onto his thighs. With a quick twist of his torso, he would flip the canoe onto his shoulders and stride up the trail, the canoe balanced above him like a gigantic green cap.

Perhaps because he was eager to get away from us for a few minutes, our guide hoisted his canoe so swiftly that we never did quite understand the physics involved in shouldering a canoe. As we tried to flip our own craft, we fell over, dropped our canoes on rocks, and committed many other atrocities against canoes and common sense. Fortunately, we were at an age when we could fumble about like that for hours and still imagine we were having a good time. Unfortunately, the fresh dents in our canoes suggested they were not nearly so flexible.

It shouldn't have been so difficult. If our guide had taken a few moments to explain the principles involved in taking a canoe from the water, we would have been able to do it with ease. Then we would have known that leverage and position, not brute strength, are the keys to hefting a canoe and carrying it across dry ground.

Landing a Canoe

By now you've brought your canoe into shore enough times that you've realized it often involves getting your feet wet. That's because you want to protect the canoe from damage it can sustain running into rocks, snags, and gravel.

When you're paddling solo, ease your canoe slowly toward land and stop the forward momentum before the bow runs aground. Test the water depth alongside the canoe with your paddle then slip your paddle onto the floor of the canoe. Hold the gunwales for balance and step over the side into the water.

Sliding one hand along the gunwale to prevent the canoe from drifting away, walk to the bow. Grasp the edge of the bow deck, then lift and pull your canoe forward until it is well up onshore.

If you're paddling with a partner, stop your canoe short of contact with the beach. The person in the bow seat steps into shallow water and holds the craft steady. The stern paddler can check the depth of the water surrounding the back of the canoe and, if it is shallow enough, step right over the side. When it is too deep, he simply moves forward, crouching and holding the gunwales, to disembark over the bow.

Parking

As you come ashore, pulling your canoe partway up the beach is a reasonably safe way to store it temporarily. At least it's easy to do when your canoe is empty. If you're traveling in a heavily-laden canoe, you may not be able to pull it onto shore. Perhaps you're on a camping trip and have weighty packs tied between the thwarts. Maybe your wildest fantasies have come true and you are returning from six months of trapping beavers in the Yukon Territory with 200 pounds of pelts heaped under the thwarts.

Instead of trying to wrestle a loaded canoe onto dry land, simply uncoil the painter and tie the end to a tree or rock. In fact, it's wise to tie the painter to something on shore even when you've beached an empty canoe. There are many sad tales of the wind pushing a canoe back onto a lake, or of the water rising and stealing an unguarded craft. It takes only a moment to knot the rope around a boulder or a branch.

Portaging

We can thank the French voyageurs of the North Country for introducing the word "portage" into our vocabulary. Although the wilderness lakes of Canada offered them passage across the continent, those watery thoroughfares were not without obstacles. The voyageurs carried the canoes from one lake to another, beating out footpaths as they went. Many of these portages were no more than a few hundred yards. Others extended for miles and were the bane of the voyaguers' existence.

When you brought your canoe to the water for the first time, you used the easiest of portaging methods. One person grasped the bow deck, the other the stern deck. You lifted the canoe and walked it to its destination. For short hauls, that's fine. Over longer distances, you'll find it tiring and awkward.

One portage method. Rest the keel on your shoulders.

Instead of holding onto the canoe as though it were a big bucket, you and your partner can lift it and rest the keel on your shoulders. It's most comfortable when you both use the shoulder on the same side.

Another carrying technique starts with the canoe on the ground and canoeists stationed at the bow and stern. They grasp the gunwales, lift the canoe, then flip it over their heads. Bearing the weight of the canoe on their hands, they are ready to walk forward.

One person can also carry an empty canoe long distances in relative comfort by using a *carrying*

Two people can carry a canoe comfortably by hoisting it over their heads.

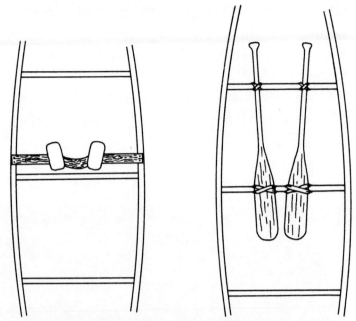

A padded yoke adds comfort to portaging (left).
Fashion a yoke out of paddles by lashing or
taping them between two thwarts.

yoke—a curved thwart spanning the center of
the craft. Some yokes are built into canoes while
others can be temporarily clamped to the gunwales. Yokes may be padded or bare wood. If you
don't have a yoke for your canoe, you can fashion
one with two paddles. Lay them across the thwarts
(see illustration) and use cord or tape to secure
them in position. The exact placement of the pad-

dles will take a little experimentation. The flat faces of the paddles should be just far enough apart to ride easily on your shoulders.

Begin by unloading everything from the canoe. Coil the painter if it is loose and tie or tape it to a

For solo portaging, one of you can help the other get under the carrying yoke.

thwart. With your partner, carry the canoe to shore and set it down. Next, roll the canoe over so the keel is up. Have your partner grasp the bow and lift the canoe as high as possible. The stern, of course, stays on the ground. While your partner holds the bow overhead, you can step underneath the canoe and, facing forward, back into the shoulder pads of the yoke or in between the paddles strapped to the thwarts. Bend at the knees and keep your back straight.

Place one hand on each gunwale and straighten up. Let the weight of the canoe settle onto your shoulders as your partner lets go of the bow. Since a properly located yoke is near the center of the canoe, the weight of the craft should be pretty well balanced. The bow will ride just a bit higher than the stern, allowing you to see where you are going.

Carrying a canoe by yourself is not difficult, although you'll quickly discover you can't make sharp turns or travel very well through branches and underbrush. Whenever you can, stick to a wide open trail. Most portage routes are well-worn and cleared of obstacles. Have your partner lead the way and alert you to changing trail conditions.

If you tire during a portage, you can rest the bow of the canoe on a low branch or in the crotch of a tree, lower the stern to the ground, and step from beneath the yoke. On some popular portage routes you'll find poles lashed between two trees at eye

Straighten up and lean forward to bring the stern of the canoe off the ground.

level, just high enough to hold the bow of a leaning canoe.

Upon reaching your destination, have your partner again take hold of the bow. Bend slowly at the knees to give up the weight of the canoe as the stern lowers to the ground. That done, step from

The voyageur method of lifting a canoe to your shoulders involves four steps. Start by pulling the craft onto your thighs.

Grab the far gunwale.

Slip your other hand around the canoe and flip
the craft over your head.

Turn and let the yoke settle onto your shoulders.

beneath the canoe and help ease the bow the rest of the way down.

When you're alone, you can use a variation of the two-person lifting technique. With the canoe on dry ground, roll it over so it's resting keel up. Grasp the bow and lift it over your head, arms extended. Carefully turn beneath the bow until you are facing forward, then work your way backwards, sliding your hands along the gunwales, until you reach the center of the canoe and feel your shoulders coming against the yoke. Rest the canoe on your shoulders, lean forward a little to lift the stern off the ground, and you're ready to move.

Reverse the procedure to get the canoe off your back. Tilt the bow up until the stern touches the ground, then hold the gunwales and take the weight of the canoe on your hands. Walk forward, scooting your hands along the gunwales until you reach the bow. With a firm grasp on the bow, step from beneath the canoe and lower it to the ground.

You might also want to try the traditional voyageur method of hoisting a canoe. It's best to practice this maneuver in shallow water so the canoe won't be damaged if you drop it. It's also helpful to have a partner spot for you.

Stand in the water on the left side of an empty canoe, midway between the bow and stern. Face the canoe and get a solid footing. Grasp the nearer gunwale with both hands and pull the canoe up onto your thighs.

With your left hand, reach across the canoe and grab the far gunwale. Next, slip your right hand as far under the canoe as you can reach so you are cradling it in your arm.

Finally, swing the canoe off your thighs and up over your head, lifting most of the weight with your right arm as you guide the canoe over with your left. Turn toward the bow so you can catch the yoke on your shoulders. If you have your hands in the right position before starting the lift, the maneuver virtually takes care of itself.

To put down the canoe, reach out around the outside of the canoe with your right arm and cradle it as you tilt it to the right off your shoulders. Ease it down to your thighs. Switch the grasp of your left hand from the far gunwale to the near one, then slide the canoe into the water or onto the ground.

Care and Maintenance— One Hour

Finish a day on the water by properly maintaining and storing your canoe and gear. You don't want to put a canoe away dirty and you don't want to store gear wet.

Before you take your canoe from the water, check for sand and grit in the bottom. If there's much of it, roll the canoe until water splashes over the gunwales. Rock it from side to side to loosen any debris, then dump out the water. A clean canoe will be more pleasant to use next time, and you're less likely to scratch the interior by grinding dirt into the finish with your shoes.

The best storage place for a canoe is a rack that holds the upside down craft off the ground. An

At the end of the day, wash out your canoe and store it properly.

aluminum canoe, practically immune to weather, can be stored outdoors with its keel toward the sky. Some canoes made of synthetic materials are subject to deterioration from long exposure to sunlight. Wood and canvas canoes and those containing wooden parts fare better indoors.

Paddles also require proper storage. A rack for them should allow them to hang straight up and down. Wooden paddles lying on damp ground or left leaning against walls may become warped.

If you have your own paddles, check them for wear after each use. A little sandpaper will smooth any roughness off the grip of wood paddles, and an application of boiled linseed oil will protect it from weathering and checking.

Inspect the joints of paddles made of plastic and metal. They must be tight. Use fine sandpaper to smooth plastic grips that have become abraded.

Life jackets should be kept in a dry, out-of-the-way place. Hanging them from cords attached to the rafters of a garage or storage shed will protect them from rodents. Good air circulation will discourage mildew and rot.

Repairing canoes generally involves a fair degree of expertise and often some specialized tools. For quick patch jobs, nothing is quite as useful as duct tape. During a day on the water, you can patch everything from a cracked paddle to a punctured canoe, and there's a high likelihood things will hold together long enough for you to get home. Clean and dry the area before applying the tape to help the adhesive hold.

Canoeing is a sport for an afternoon—and for a lifetime!

It's always best to attend to serious damage before you take the canoe out again. If it is a rental craft, bring the problem to the attention of the owner.

*   *   *   *

As you can see, learning to canoe is not very difficult. One day on the water has given you the basic skills you need to paddle safely and well. It also has provided a taste of the joys of paddling, and a hint of adventures to come.

Canoeing is a sport for an afternoon, and for a lifetime. The hours you spend on the water will be refreshing, challenging, and utterly satisfying. The time to start is now.

Good luck and good paddling!

Index

101